Optimal Living

Transform Your Life and Achieve True Happiness: A Comprehensive Guide to Optimal Living for Mind, Body, and Soul

Lance P. Richards

Optimal Living: Transform Your Life and Achieve True Happiness: A Comprehensive Guide to Optimal Living for Mind, Body, and Soul

Table of Contents

01: Introduction: Understanding Optimal Living................1

02: Mindset: The Key to Optimal Living....................8

03: Setting Goals for Optimal Living....................11

04: The Power of Positive Thinking....................15

05: Overcoming Negative Thoughts and Emotions............19

06: Mindfulness and Meditation for Optimal Living.........23

07: Stress Management Techniques for Optimal Living.....27

08: Building Resilience for Optimal Living...............31

09: Self-Care for Optimal Living.......................36

10: Building Confidence for Optimal Living...............39

11: Developing Positive Relationships for Optimal Living..43

12: Communication Skills for Optimal Living..............47

13: Building a Support System for Optimal Living............50

14: Physical Health for Optimal Living................53

15: The Importance of Sleep for Optimal Living.............56

16: Nutrition for Optimal Living.......................59

17: Exercise for Optimal Living.......................62

18: Managing Chronic Illness for Optimal Living............66

19: Mental Health for Optimal Living...................70

20: Overcoming Anxiety for Optimal Living...............74

21: Overcoming Depression for Optimal Living...............78

22: Coping with Trauma for Optimal Living...............83

23: Building Emotional Intelligence for Optimal Living....86

24: Building a Growth Mindset for Optimal Living...........90

25: Building a Strong Work Ethic for Optimal Living........93

26: Finding Work-Life Balance for Optimal Living...........97

27: Building a Strong Financial Foundation for Optimal Living..102

28: Creating a Happy Home for Optimal Living...............107

29: Building Strong Parenting Skills for Optimal Living...112

30: Building Strong Marriage and Relationships for Optimal Living..115

31: Building Strong Friendships for Optimal Living..........117

32: Building Strong Relationships with Extended Family for Optimal Living..120

33: Building a Strong Community for Optimal Living......123

34: Finding Your Purpose in Life for Optimal Living.......126

35: Building a Strong Spiritual Foundation for Optimal Living..129

36: Conclusion: Achieving True Happiness Through Optimal Living..132

Thank You..135

Disclaimer..136

01: Introduction: Understanding Optimal Living

Introduction: Understanding Optimal Living

Optimal living is a concept that refers to living a life that is fulfilling, happy, and healthy in all aspects, including mind, body, and soul. It is about striving for excellence and reaching your full potential, both physically and mentally. By living an optimal life, you can enjoy all the benefits that come with a balanced, harmonious existence. In this comprehensive guide, we will explore the many different aspects of optimal living and provide you with practical tips and advice to help you transform your life and achieve true happiness.

The concept of optimal living is not new, but it has become increasingly popular in recent years as people seek to escape the stresses and demands of modern life and achieve a sense of balance and well-being. Optimal living is not just about physical health and fitness, although these are important components. It also encompasses mental health, relationships, work-life balance, financial stability, spirituality, and much more. In other words, optimal living is about creating a life that is complete and fulfilling in every way.

01: INTRODUCTION: UNDERSTANDING OPTIMAL LIVING

At its core, optimal living is about taking control of your life and choosing to live it on your terms. It is about breaking free from the constraints of society and embracing a life that is true to your values and beliefs. By living an optimal life, you can enjoy greater happiness, fulfillment, and purpose, and avoid many of the negative effects of modern living, such as stress, anxiety, depression, and burnout.

In this chapter, we will explore what optimal living is and why it is important. We will also look at the key elements of optimal living and the benefits that come with embracing this way of life. Whether you are looking to improve your physical health, your mental well-being, your relationships, or your overall happiness, this comprehensive guide will provide you with the tools and resources you need to achieve your goals.

So, what exactly is optimal living?

Optimal living is a holistic approach to life that focuses on creating a balance and harmony in all areas of life, including mind, body, and soul. It is about finding a way to live life to the fullest, to reach your full potential, and to experience the joy and happiness that comes with a well-lived life. Optimal living is not just about doing one or two things well, but about doing many things well and in a balanced way.

In order to live an optimal life, you need to focus on several key areas, including:

– Mindset: Your mindset is your mental attitude and outlook on life. A positive, growth-oriented mindset is essential for optimal living, as it allows you to overcome obstacles and challenges, and to see opportunities and possibilities where others may see only limitations.

– Goals: Setting goals for yourself is an important part of optimal living, as it gives you something to work towards and provides you with a sense of purpose and direction. Goals can be personal, professional, or a combination of both, and should be meaningful, achievable, and aligned with your values and beliefs.

– Health: Physical health is a critical component of optimal living, as it affects your energy, mood, and overall well-being. A healthy diet, regular exercise, and adequate sleep are essential for optimal living, and can help you to avoid many of the negative effects of modern living, such as stress, anxiety, and burnout.

– Relationships: Building strong relationships with others is a critical component of optimal living, as it provides you with support, love, and connection. Whether you are looking to strengthen your marriage, your parenting skills, your friendships, or your extended family relationships, it is important to invest time and effort into building strong and meaningful connections with others.

– Work-life balance: Balancing work and life is an essential part of optimal living, as it helps to reduce stress and improve well-being. This may involve finding a job that aligns with your values and beliefs, setting boundaries between work and personal time, and finding ways to integrate work and life in a healthy and fulfilling way.

– Personal development: Optimal living is about continuously growing and improving, both personally and professionally. This may involve learning new skills, taking on new challenges, and embracing new experiences. By embracing a growth mindset and seeking out new opportunities for personal development, you can continue to grow and evolve throughout your life.

01: INTRODUCTION: UNDERSTANDING OPTIMAL LIVING

– Spirituality: Spirituality is a personal and often intimate aspect of optimal living, and can provide a sense of meaning, purpose, and connection to something greater than oneself. Whether through religious practice, meditation, or mindfulness, spirituality can play a critical role in helping to provide a sense of balance and well-being in life.

These are just a few of the key elements of optimal living, and there are many others as well. The most important thing is to find what works for you, and to make a conscious effort to create a balanced and fulfilling life that is true to your values and beliefs.

So, what are the benefits of optimal living?

There are many benefits to living an optimal life, including:

– Increased happiness and fulfillment: Optimal living can help to increase happiness and fulfillment, as it provides a sense of purpose, direction, and meaning in life. By focusing on personal growth and well-being, you can enjoy a more positive outlook on life and experience greater happiness and joy.

01: INTRODUCTION: UNDERSTANDING OPTIMAL LIVING

– Improved physical health: A focus on physical health is an essential part of optimal living, and can help to improve energy, mood, and overall well-being. By embracing a healthy diet and regular exercise, you can avoid many of the negative effects of modern living, such as stress and burnout, and enjoy better health and wellness.

– Stronger relationships: Building strong relationships with others is a critical component of optimal living, and can provide a sense of love, connection, and support. Whether you are looking to strengthen your marriage, your parenting skills, or your friendships, investing time and effort into building strong and meaningful connections with others can have a profound impact on your life.

– Better work-life balance: Optimal living is about finding balance in all areas of life, including work and personal time. By setting boundaries between work and life and finding ways to integrate work and life in a healthy and fulfilling way, you can avoid the negative effects of burnout and enjoy greater happiness and well-being.

– Increased personal growth: Optimal living is about continuously growing and improving, both personally and professionally. By embracing a growth mindset and seeking out new opportunities for personal development, you can continue to grow and evolve throughout your life, and enjoy greater happiness and fulfillment.

In conclusion, optimal living is a holistic approach to life that focuses on creating balance and harmony in all areas of life, including mind, body, and soul. It is about taking control of your life and choosing to live it on your terms, and about embracing a life that is true to your values and beliefs. Whether you are looking to improve your physical health, your mental well-being, your relationships, or your overall happiness, this comprehensive guide will provide you with the tools and resources you need to achieve your goals and transform your life.

02: Mindset: The Key to Optimal Living

One of the most critical components of optimal living is having the right mindset. Your mindset is essentially the way you view and approach the world around you, and it has a profound impact on your happiness, success, and overall well-being. Whether you are looking to improve your physical health, your relationships, or your overall happiness, having the right mindset is essential. In this chapter, we will explore the key elements of a positive and empowering mindset, and how you can develop one for yourself.

– The power of a growth mindset: A growth mindset is the belief that you can grow, change, and improve, no matter what obstacles you may face. This type of mindset is characterized by a focus on personal growth, a willingness to embrace challenges, and a belief in the power of hard work and perseverance. By embracing a growth mindset, you can overcome obstacles and achieve your goals, no matter how difficult they may seem.

– Overcoming limiting beliefs: Limiting beliefs are negative thoughts and attitudes that hold you back and prevent you from reaching your full potential. Common limiting beliefs include beliefs about your abilities, your worth, and your potential for success. To overcome limiting beliefs, it is essential to become aware of them, challenge them, and replace them with positive and empowering beliefs.

– The power of positive self-talk: Positive self-talk is an essential component of a positive mindset, and it involves speaking to yourself in a positive and encouraging way. This type of self-talk can help to boost your confidence, reduce stress, and improve your overall well-being. By making a conscious effort to practice positive self-talk, you can develop a more positive and empowering mindset, and enjoy greater happiness and success in life.

– The importance of gratitude: Gratitude is the practice of recognizing and appreciating the good things in your life. This can include simple things like the beauty of nature, the love of your friends and family, and the opportunities that you have been given. By developing a daily gratitude practice, you can cultivate a more positive and optimistic outlook on life, and enjoy greater happiness and well-being.

– Embracing change: Change is inevitable, and it can be difficult to navigate at times. However, by embracing change, you can develop greater resilience and flexibility, and be better equipped to handle challenges as they arise. By embracing change, you can also create new opportunities for growth and success, and transform your life in meaningful and positive ways.

– The importance of mindfulness: Mindfulness is the practice of being present in the moment, and it is an essential component of a positive and empowering mindset. By practicing mindfulness, you can reduce stress, improve your focus and attention, and cultivate greater self-awareness and inner peace. Whether you choose to practice mindfulness through meditation, yoga, or simply taking a few deep breaths, incorporating mindfulness into your daily routine can help you to develop a more positive and empowering mindset.

In conclusion, developing a positive and empowering mindset is an essential part of optimal living. By embracing a growth mindset, overcoming limiting beliefs, practicing positive self-talk, developing gratitude, embracing change, and incorporating mindfulness into your daily routine, you can cultivate a more positive outlook on life, and enjoy greater happiness, success, and well-being.

03: Setting Goals for Optimal Living

Setting goals is an essential step in achieving optimal living, as it gives you a clear direction and purpose in life. By setting achievable and meaningful goals, you can transform your life, improve your well-being, and achieve true happiness. In this chapter, we will explore the key elements of goal-setting and provide you with tips and strategies for setting and achieving your goals.

– The importance of goal-setting: Goal-setting is an important tool for helping you achieve optimal living, as it provides you with a clear sense of direction and purpose. When you set goals, you are able to focus your efforts, increase your motivation, and measure your progress. Additionally, goal-setting can also help you to stay accountable and stay on track, even when faced with obstacles and setbacks.

– SMART goal-setting: When it comes to setting goals, it is essential to use the SMART goal-setting framework. SMART goals are Specific, Measurable, Achievable, Relevant, and Time-bound. By following this framework, you can ensure that your goals are clear, achievable, and relevant to your overall well-being. Additionally, SMART goals help you to track your progress and stay motivated, as you can see how far you have come and how much closer you are to achieving your goals.

– Setting realistic and achievable goals: When setting goals, it is important to make sure that they are achievable and realistic. By setting achievable goals, you can avoid disappointment and frustration, and feel a sense of accomplishment and satisfaction as you work towards your goals. Additionally, setting realistic goals can help you to build momentum and stay motivated, as you see progress and experience success along the way.

– Setting goals in different areas of your life: To achieve optimal living, it is important to set goals in different areas of your life, including physical health, mental and emotional well-being, relationships, personal growth, and career and finances. By setting goals in different areas of your life, you can ensure that you are working towards a well-rounded and fulfilling life, and that all aspects of your life are contributing to your overall happiness and well-being.

– Breaking down larger goals into smaller, achievable steps:

When setting goals, it can be helpful to break down larger goals into smaller, achievable steps. This can help you to avoid feeling overwhelmed and discouraged, and it can also help you to track your progress and stay motivated. Additionally, breaking down larger goals into smaller steps can help you to focus on taking action, and to develop new habits and routines that will support your progress towards your goals.

– The power of visualizing success: Visualizing success is an important component of goal-setting, and it involves imagining yourself as having already achieved your goals. By visualizing success, you can increase your motivation, build confidence, and develop a more positive and empowering mindset. Additionally, visualization can also help you to stay focused and committed to your goals, even when faced with obstacles and setbacks.

In conclusion, goal-setting is an essential component of optimal living, as it provides you with a clear sense of direction and purpose, and helps you to stay motivated and committed to your goals. By following the SMART goal-setting framework, setting achievable and realistic goals, breaking down larger goals into smaller steps, and visualizing success, you can transform your life and achieve true happiness.

04: The Power of Positive Thinking

In the quest for optimal living, one of the most important things to consider is our mindset and how we approach life's challenges and opportunities. Our thoughts have a profound impact on our happiness and well-being, and adopting a positive outlook can transform our lives in ways that we may have never thought possible. In this chapter, we will delve into the power of positive thinking and how you can use it to achieve true happiness and fulfillment.

What is Positive Thinking?

Positive thinking is the practice of focusing on the good in any situation and looking for solutions rather than dwelling on problems. It involves adopting an optimistic outlook, seeing challenges as opportunities for growth, and embracing a growth mindset that embraces change and progress. Positive thinking is about more than just being happy; it's about feeling empowered, motivated, and in control of your life.

The Benefits of Positive Thinking

04: THE POWER OF POSITIVE THINKING

Positive thinking has been shown to have a range of benefits for our mental, emotional, and physical health. These benefits include:

– Improved Mental Health: Positive thinking has been shown to reduce stress, anxiety, and depression and improve overall mental health. When we focus on the good in any situation, we are less likely to get bogged down by negative thoughts and emotions that can contribute to mental health issues.

– Increased Resilience: Positive thinking helps us develop resilience in the face of challenges and setbacks. When we have a positive outlook, we are more likely to bounce back from difficult situations and view them as opportunities for growth and improvement.

– Better Relationships: Positive thinking can help improve our relationships with others. When we are positive and optimistic, we are more likely to attract positive people into our lives and have better relationships with those we already know.

– Improved Physical Health: Positive thinking has been shown to improve physical health as well. Studies have shown that positive thinking can boost the immune system, reduce inflammation, and improve heart health.

– Increased Productivity and Success: Positive thinking can also lead to increased productivity and success. When we have a positive outlook, we are more likely to take action and pursue our goals with confidence and determination.

How to Adopt a Positive Mindset

Adopting a positive mindset is a lifelong journey, but there are many practical steps you can take to get started. These include:

– Practice gratitude: Make a habit of focusing on what you are grateful for each day. This can be as simple as taking a few minutes each day to write down a list of things you are thankful for.

– Surround yourself with positive people: Seek out positive, supportive people who will encourage and inspire you. Avoid spending time with those who bring you down or are negative.

– Embrace positive self-talk: Pay attention to the self-talk in your head and make an effort to replace negative thoughts with positive ones.

– Practice mindfulness: Mindfulness is the practice of being present and fully engaged in the moment. It can help you cultivate a positive outlook by reducing stress and increasing gratitude and self-awareness.

– Focus on solutions: When faced with challenges, focus on finding solutions rather than dwelling on problems. This will help you maintain a positive outlook and find creative ways to overcome obstacles.

In conclusion, the power of positive thinking cannot be overstated. By adopting a positive outlook and focusing on the good in any situation, you can transform your life and achieve true happiness and fulfillment. So, start today and embrace the power of positive thinking as you journey towards optimal living.

05: Overcoming Negative Thoughts and Emotions

One of the biggest obstacles to achieving optimal living is the presence of negative thoughts and emotions that can hold us back and prevent us from reaching our full potential. These negative thoughts and emotions can come in many forms, such as self-doubt, anxiety, fear, and anger. However, the good news is that with the right tools and strategies, it is possible to overcome these negative thoughts and emotions and cultivate a positive and empowering mindset. In this chapter, we will explore some of the most effective methods for overcoming negative thoughts and emotions and achieving true happiness and well-being.

Understand the Source of Negative Thoughts and Emotions

The first step in overcoming negative thoughts and emotions is to understand their source. Often, these negative thoughts and emotions are rooted in past experiences, childhood memories, or deeply held beliefs and fears. By gaining insight into the root cause of these negative thoughts and emotions, we can begin to address them and make meaningful changes to our mindset and behavior.

05: OVERCOMING NEGATIVE THOUGHTS AND EMO- TIONS

Develop a Growth Mindset

Adopting a growth mindset is an effective way to overcome negative thoughts and emotions. A growth mindset involves embracing change, viewing challenges as opportunities for growth, and being open to new experiences and ideas. When we have a growth mindset, we are less likely to be held back by negative thoughts and emotions and more likely to view obstacles as opportunities for growth and improvement.

Practice Mindfulness

Mindfulness is the practice of being fully present and engaged in the moment, without judgment or distraction. This powerful tool can help us overcome negative thoughts and emotions by reducing stress, improving self-awareness, and promoting positive self-talk. By becoming more mindful, we can learn to live in the present moment, appreciate the beauty around us, and cultivate a more positive outlook on life.

Challenge Negative Thoughts

05: OVERCOMING NEGATIVE THOUGHTS AND EMOTIONS

Another effective strategy for overcoming negative thoughts and emotions is to challenge them directly. When negative thoughts arise, take a moment to examine them and ask yourself if they are true and helpful. Often, we find that negative thoughts are based on false beliefs and assumptions, and when we challenge them, we can gain a more accurate and positive perspective.

Focus on Gratitude

Focusing on gratitude is another effective tool for overcoming negative thoughts and emotions. When we focus on the things we are grateful for, we are less likely to dwell on negative thoughts and emotions and more likely to see the good in any situation. By developing a gratitude practice, we can cultivate a positive outlook and foster greater happiness and well-being.

Practice Self-Compassion

Self-compassion is the practice of treating ourselves with the same kindness, care, and understanding that we would offer to a close friend. By practicing self-compassion, we can overcome negative thoughts and emotions by shifting our focus from self-criticism and judgment to self-care and understanding. This powerful tool can help us develop greater self-awareness and self-love, which are essential for achieving optimal living.

In conclusion, overcoming negative thoughts and emotions is an essential part of the journey towards optimal living. By understanding the source of these negative thoughts and emotions, adopting a growth mindset, practicing mindfulness, challenging negative thoughts, focusing on gratitude, and practicing self-compassion, we can cultivate a positive and empowering mindset that will help us achieve true happiness and well-being. So, embrace these tools and strategies and start your journey towards optimal living today!

06: Mindfulness and Meditation for Optimal Living

Mindfulness and meditation are powerful tools that can help us achieve optimal living by reducing stress, promoting self-awareness, and fostering positive emotions. These ancient practices have been used for thousands of years to promote physical, emotional, and mental well-being, and they are just as relevant and beneficial today as they were in the past. In this chapter, we will explore the benefits of mindfulness and meditation and how they can be used to achieve optimal living for mind, body, and soul.

What is Mindfulness?

Mindfulness is the practice of being fully present and engaged in the moment, without judgment or distraction. This simple yet powerful technique can help us reduce stress, improve focus, and cultivate greater self-awareness. By becoming more mindful, we can learn to live in the present moment, appreciate the beauty around us, and cultivate a more positive outlook on life.

What is Meditation?

06: MINDFULNESS AND MEDITATION FOR OPTIMAL LIVING

Meditation is a practice that involves focusing the mind and reducing distractions, with the goal of achieving greater mental clarity, emotional stability, and physical relaxation. Meditation can be performed in many different ways, including mindfulness meditation, guided visualization, and mantra meditation. Regardless of the form it takes, meditation is a powerful tool for reducing stress, improving focus, and promoting well-being.

Benefits of Mindfulness and Meditation

There are many benefits to practicing mindfulness and meditation, including:

– Reduced stress and anxiety: Mindfulness and meditation can help to reduce stress and anxiety by promoting relaxation and reducing the physical and mental symptoms of stress.

– Improved focus and concentration: By training the mind to focus and reduce distractions, mindfulness and meditation can improve focus and concentration, making it easier to achieve goals and complete tasks.

06: MINDFULNESS AND MEDITATION FOR OPTIMAL LIVING

– Greater self-awareness: Mindfulness and meditation can help us become more aware of our thoughts, emotions, and behavior, allowing us to make changes that promote well-being.

– Improved sleep: Mindfulness and meditation can help to improve sleep by reducing stress and promoting relaxation.

– Increased happiness and well-being: By reducing stress and promoting positive emotions, mindfulness and meditation can help to increase happiness and well-being, promoting optimal living for mind, body, and soul.

Getting Started with Mindfulness and Meditation

Getting started with mindfulness and meditation is easy and accessible, and it can be done from the comfort of your own home. Here are some tips to get started:

– Set aside time each day: Make time each day for mindfulness and meditation, even if it is just a few minutes. You can do this first thing in the morning, before bed, or at any other time that works for you.

– Find a quiet, comfortable space: Find a quiet, comfortable space where you can sit or lie down and practice mindfulness and meditation without distraction.

– Focus on your breath: One of the simplest and most effective mindfulness practices is to simply focus on your breath. Pay attention to the sensation of the air entering and leaving your body, and allow your mind to relax and release any stress or tension.

– Start with guided meditations: If you are new to meditation, consider starting with guided meditations, which can be found online or in app form. Guided meditations can help you get started and provide structure and support as you develop your meditation practice.

In conclusion, mindfulness and meditation are powerful tools for achieving optimal living for mind, body, and soul. By reducing stress, promoting self-awareness, and fostering positive emotions, these ancient practices can help us achieve greater happiness and well-being. So, start incorporating mindfulness and meditation into your daily routine today and experience the many benefits for yourself

07: Stress Management Techniques for Optimal Living

Stress is an inevitable part of life, but it doesn't have to control us. By learning stress management techniques, we can take control of our stress and use it as a tool for growth and improvement. In this chapter, we will explore the various stress management techniques that can be used to achieve optimal living for mind, body, and soul.

Understanding Stress

Stress is a normal physical and emotional response to challenging situations or events. It is a survival mechanism that prepares the body and mind to respond to danger. In small doses, stress can be helpful, motivating us to take action and get things done. But when stress becomes chronic and overwhelming, it can have negative impacts on our health, relationships, and well-being.

The Negative Effects of Chronic Stress

Chronic stress can have many negative effects, including:

– Physical symptoms, such as headaches, muscle tension, and fatigue

07: STRESS MANAGEMENT TECHNIQUES FOR OP-TIMAL LIVING

– Mental health issues, such as anxiety, depression, and irritability

– Poor sleep and decreased ability to concentrate

– Decreased immune function

– Increased risk of heart disease and stroke

– Stress Management Techniques

Fortunately, there are many stress management techniques that can help us take control of our stress and promote optimal living. Some of the most effective techniques include:

– Exercise: Exercise is one of the best stress management techniques, as it helps to release tension, improve mood, and increase endorphins. Aim to exercise for at least 30 minutes each day, and consider incorporating mindfulness into your workout routine.

– Mindfulness and meditation: Mindfulness and meditation, as discussed in Chapter 7, can help reduce stress and promote relaxation, and are some of the most effective stress management techniques.

07: STRESS MANAGEMENT TECHNIQUES FOR OP-
TIMAL LIVING

– Deep breathing: Deep breathing is a simple yet powerful stress management technique that can be done anywhere, anytime. Simply take a deep breath in through your nose and slowly exhale through your mouth, repeating several times.

– Progressive muscle relaxation: Progressive muscle relaxation is a technique that involves tensing and relaxing different muscle groups to help release tension and promote relaxation.

– Time management: Good time management can help reduce stress by reducing the sense of being overwhelmed and helping us prioritize our tasks and responsibilities.

– Seeking support: Sometimes, talking to a trusted friend, family member, or mental health professional can help us manage stress and find new perspectives.

– Healthy habits: Maintaining healthy habits, such as eating well, getting enough sleep, and avoiding unhealthy substances, can help reduce stress and promote optimal living.

In conclusion, stress is a normal and inevitable part of life,

but it doesn't have to control us. By using stress management techniques, such as exercise, mindfulness and meditation, deep breathing, progressive muscle relaxation, time
management, seeking support, and maintaining healthy
habits, we can take control of our stress and achieve optimal
living for mind, body, and soul.

08: Building Resilience for Optimal Living

Resilience is the ability to bounce back from adversity and challenges. It allows us to face difficult situations with strength and determination, and to come out the other side even stronger. In this chapter, we will explore the key elements of resilience and how to build resilience for optimal living.

What is Resilience?

Resilience is the ability to adapt to change and challenges, and to maintain or regain a positive outlook, even in the face of adversity. It is the capacity to recover quickly from setbacks and to continue pursuing our goals and aspirations, despite challenges and obstacles.

Why is Resilience Important for Optimal Living?

Resilience is crucial for optimal living, as it helps us to:

– Overcome adversity and challenges

– Maintain a positive outlook and perspective

– Pursue our goals and aspirations, despite obstacles

– Improve our physical and mental health

– Build stronger relationships and connections with others

Key Elements of Resilience

The following are key elements of resilience that can help us build resilience and achieve optimal living:

– Positive outlook: A positive outlook can help us maintain a sense of hope and optimism, even in the face of adversity.

– Flexibility: Flexibility allows us to adapt to change and challenges, and to find new and innovative solutions to problems.

– Problem-solving skills: Problem-solving skills help us to find creative and effective solutions to challenges and obstacles.

– Strong support network: Having a strong support network of friends, family, and professionals can provide us with the support and encouragement we need to overcome challenges and adversity.

– Self-care: Self-care is essential for building resilience, as it helps us to maintain our physical and mental health, and to manage stress and adversity.

– Mindfulness and meditation: Mindfulness and meditation, as discussed in Chapter 7, can help us develop a greater sense of awareness, calm, and resilience in the face of adversity.

– Gratitude and appreciation: Cultivating gratitude and appreciation can help us maintain a positive outlook and focus on the good in our lives, even in difficult times.

Building Resilience

The following are some practical strategies for building resilience and achieving optimal living:

– Set achievable goals: Setting achievable goals and breaking them down into manageable steps can help us maintain a sense of purpose and direction, even in the face of adversity.

– Practice self-compassion: Treating ourselves with kindness and compassion, even when we make mistakes or face setbacks, can help us build resilience and overcome adversity.

— Seek support: Seeking support from friends, family, or mental health professionals can provide us with the encouragement and support we need to overcome challenges and adversity.

— Take care of your physical health: Regular exercise, healthy eating, and getting enough sleep can help us maintain our physical and mental health, and build resilience.

— Learn from adversity: Reflecting on our experiences and learning from our setbacks and challenges can help us build resilience and grow stronger from adversity.

— Cultivate gratitude and appreciation: Regularly expressing gratitude and appreciation for the good in our lives can help us maintain a positive outlook, even in difficult times.

In conclusion, resilience is a key element of optimal living, allowing us to overcome adversity and challenges, maintain a positive outlook, and pursue our goals and aspirations. By cultivating a positive outlook, flexibility, problem-solving skills, a strong support network, self-care, mindfulness and meditation, gratitude, and appreciation, we can build resilience and achieve optimal living for mind, body, and soul.

09: Self-Care for Optimal Living

Self-care is the deliberate and intentional practice of taking care of oneself, both physically and emotionally. In this chapter, we will explore the importance of self-care for optimal living and provide practical tips for incorporating self-care into your daily life.

What is Self-Care?

Self-care is the practice of taking care of oneself, including both physical and emotional well-being. It is about putting oneself first, in a healthy and balanced way, and prioritizing self-care in order to improve one's overall well-being.

Why is Self-Care Important for Optimal Living?

Self-care is essential for optimal living, as it helps us to:

– Maintain our physical and emotional well-being

– Reduce stress and improve our ability to manage stress

– Improve our relationships and connections with others

– Increase our productivity and creativity

– Boost our confidence and self-esteem

Types of Self-Care

Self-care can take many different forms, including:

– Physical self-care: This includes activities that promote physical well-being, such as exercise, healthy eating, and getting enough sleep.

– Emotional self-care: This includes activities that promote emotional well-being, such as journaling, meditation, and therapy.

– Mental self-care: This includes activities that promote mental well-being, such as engaging in hobbies, reading, and spending time with loved ones.

– Spiritual self-care: This includes activities that promote spiritual well-being, such as prayer, mindfulness, and connecting with nature.

Incorporating Self-Care into Your Daily Life

Incorporating self-care into your daily life can be challenging, especially when you have a busy schedule. However, there are many simple and effective ways to prioritize self-care, including:

– Make time for self-care: Set aside time each day for self-care, whether it's 15 minutes in the morning, or an hour in the evening.

– Experiment with different types of self-care: Try different types of self-care, such as physical, emotional, mental, and spiritual self-care, to find what works best for you.

– Make self-care a priority: Prioritize self-care, just as you would any other important appointment or commitment.

– Get support: Ask friends and family to support your self-care efforts, or seek support from a therapist or coach.

– Celebrate your successes: Celebrate your self-care successes, no matter how small, to reinforce the importance of self-care in your life.

In conclusion, self-care is an essential component of optimal living, allowing us to maintain our physical and emotional well-being, reduce stress, and improve our relationships and connections with others. By incorporating self-care into your daily life, and prioritizing self-care as a top priority, you can achieve true happiness and optimal living for mind, body, and soul.

10: Building Confidence for Optimal Living

Confidence is the belief in one's abilities, qualities, and judgment. It plays a significant role in our overall well-being and can greatly impact our happiness and success in life. In this chapter, we will discuss the importance of confidence for optimal living and provide practical tips for building and maintaining confidence.

What is Confidence?

Confidence is the belief in one's abilities, qualities, and judgment. It is the feeling of being self-assured and capable, and the trust in oneself to handle challenges and succeed in life. Confidence is not the same as arrogance, which is the belief in one's superiority over others. Confidence is about self-acceptance and belief in oneself, without diminishing the worth of others.

Why is Confidence Important for Optimal Living?

Confidence is important for optimal living because it:

– Increases our sense of self-worth and self-esteem

– Improves our ability to handle challenges and stress

– Increases our resilience in the face of adversity

– Increases our motivation and drive

– Improves our relationships and connections with others

Tips for Building Confidence

Building confidence takes time and effort, but it is well worth it. Here are some practical tips for building and maintaining confidence:

– Practice self-care: Engage in self-care activities that promote physical, emotional, mental, and spiritual well-being.

– Set achievable goals: Set achievable goals for yourself and work towards them, celebrating your successes along the way.

– Surround yourself with positive people: Surround yourself with positive and supportive people who uplift and encourage you.

– Practice self-affirmations: Repeat positive affirmations to yourself regularly, to reinforce the belief in your abilities and qualities.

– Learn from failure: Embrace failure as a learning opportunity, rather than a reflection of your worth.

– Focus on your strengths: Focus on your strengths, and actively work to develop them.

– Take action: Take action towards your goals, no matter how small the steps may be. The more action you take, the more confident you will become.

Maintaining Confidence

Maintaining confidence requires ongoing effort and intentional practices. Here are some tips for maintaining confidence:

– Practice gratitude: Cultivate an attitude of gratitude, focusing on what you have, rather than what you don't have.

– Stay positive: Stay positive, and actively work to reframe negative thoughts and beliefs.

– Surround yourself with positive influences: Surround

yourself with positive influences, such as books, movies, and people, that uplift and encourage you.

– Celebrate your successes: Celebrate your successes, no matter how small, to reinforce the belief in your abilities and qualities.

– Forgive yourself: Forgive yourself for your mistakes, and move forward with a positive attitude.

In conclusion, confidence is an essential component of optimal living, as it increases our sense of self-worth, improves our ability to handle challenges and stress, and improves our relationships and connections with others. By building and maintaining confidence, through self-care, goal-setting, and positive influences, you can achieve true happiness and optimal living for mind, body, and soul.

11: Developing Positive Relationships for Optimal Living

Positive relationships with others are crucial for our overall well-being and happiness. In this chapter, we will discuss the importance of positive relationships for optimal living, and provide practical tips for developing and maintaining positive relationships.

What are Positive Relationships?

Positive relationships are relationships that bring joy, fulfillment, and support to our lives. They are characterized by mutual respect, trust, kindness, and support. Positive relationships can exist in many forms, such as romantic relationships, friendships, family relationships, and professional relationships.

Why are Positive Relationships Important for Optimal Living?

Positive relationships are important for optimal living because they:

– Provide emotional support and comfort

11: DEVELOPING POSITIVE RELATIONSHIPS FOR OPTIMAL LIVING

– Increase feelings of happiness and fulfillment

– Improve physical and mental health

– Reduce stress and anxiety

– Strengthen the sense of belonging and community

Tips for Developing Positive Relationships

Developing positive relationships requires effort and intentional practices. Here are some tips for developing positive relationships:

– Practice empathy: Try to understand and respect others' perspectives, emotions, and experiences.

– Be honest and authentic: Be honest and authentic with others, and build relationships based on trust and respect.

– Be open and communicative: Encourage open and effective communication, and actively listen to others.

– Show gratitude and appreciation: Show gratitude and appreciation for others, and express your feelings and emotions.

– Be supportive and encouraging: Be supportive and encouraging to others, and offer help and guidance when needed.

– Practice forgiveness: Forgive others for their mistakes, and let go of grudges and negative emotions.

Maintaining Positive Relationships

Maintaining positive relationships requires ongoing effort and intentional practices. Here are some tips for maintaining positive relationships:

– Continuously communicate: Continuously communicate with others, and actively listen to their perspectives, emotions, and experiences.

– Show kindness and respect: Show kindness and respect to others, and treat them with dignity and empathy.

– Celebrate milestones and successes: Celebrate milestones and successes with others, and share in their joy and happiness.

– Resolve conflicts constructively: Resolve conflicts constructively, and work towards finding mutually beneficial solutions.

– Be flexible and adaptable: Be flexible and adaptable, and be willing to make adjustments and compromises in relationships.

In conclusion, positive relationships are crucial for optimal living, as they provide emotional support, increase feelings of happiness and fulfillment, and improve physical and mental health. By developing and maintaining positive relationships, through empathy, honesty, communication, and kindness, you can achieve true happiness and optimal living for mind, body, and soul.

12: Communication Skills for Optimal Living

Effective communication is a critical component of optimal living, as it allows us to connect with others, build positive relationships, and express our thoughts, feelings, and needs. In this chapter, we will discuss the importance of communication skills for optimal living, and provide practical tips for improving your communication skills.

What are Communication Skills?

Communication skills are the abilities we use to express ourselves effectively, understand others, and interact in a way that promotes positive relationships and understanding. Communication skills involve listening, speaking, reading, and writing.

Why are Communication Skills Important for Optimal Living?

Effective communication skills are important for optimal living because they:

– Foster positive relationships with others

– Promote understanding and empathy

– Increase personal and professional success

– Reduce conflict and misunderstandings

– Improve mental and emotional well-being

Tips for Improving Communication Skills

Improving communication skills requires effort and intentional practices. Here are some tips for improving your communication skills:

– Listen actively: Focus on what others are saying, and actively listen to their perspectives, emotions, and experiences.

– Speak clearly and concisely: Speak clearly and concisely, and express your thoughts, feelings, and needs effectively.

– Use non-verbal communication: Use non-verbal communication, such as body language and facial expressions, to enhance your message.

– Practice active listening: Practice active listening, and avoid interrupting or speaking over others.

12: COMMUNICATION SKILLS FOR OPTIMAL LIVING

– Express empathy: Express empathy and understanding, and show interest in others' perspectives, emotions, and experiences.

– Ask questions: Ask questions to clarify understanding and seek additional information.

– Write effectively: Write clearly and concisely, and express your thoughts, feelings, and needs effectively in written form.

– Manage stress and anxiety: Manage stress and anxiety, as it can affect your ability to communicate effectively.

In conclusion, effective communication skills are crucial for optimal living, as they foster positive relationships, promote understanding and empathy, and improve mental and emotional well-being. By developing and improving your communication skills, you can achieve true happiness and optimal living for mind, body, and soul.

13: Building a Support System for Optimal Living

Having a strong support system is essential for achieving optimal living and true happiness. A support system is a group of people who provide emotional, social, and practical support to help you navigate life's challenges and overcome obstacles. In this chapter, we will discuss the importance of building a support system and provide practical tips for doing so.

Why is a Support System Important for Optimal Living?

A support system is important for optimal living because it:

– Provides emotional support during difficult times

– Offers a sense of belonging and connectedness

– Offers practical help and resources when needed

– Increases self-esteem and confidence

– Improves mental and emotional well-being

How to Build a Support System

13: BUILDING A SUPPORT SYSTEM FOR OPTIMAL LIVING

Building a support system takes time and effort, but it is a valuable investment in your mental and emotional well-being. Here are some practical tips for building a support system:

– Connect with friends and family: Maintain strong relationships with friends and family, and reach out to them for support when needed.

– Join social groups: Join social groups, such as clubs, organizations, or hobbies, to connect with others who share similar interests.

– Seek professional help: Seek professional help, such as a therapist or counselor, to receive support and guidance when needed.

– Volunteer and give back: Volunteer and give back to others, as it can provide a sense of purpose and connectedness.

– Surround yourself with positive people: Surround yourself with positive and supportive people, and avoid those who bring negativity into your life.

– Build a network of support: Build a network of support by

reaching out to friends, family, and other supportive individuals.

– Stay open to new relationships: Stay open to new relationships and be willing to form new connections.

– Practice self-care: Practice self-care and engage in activities that help you recharge and refresh, such as exercise, meditation, or spending time in nature.

In conclusion, building a strong support system is critical for optimal living and true happiness. By reaching out to friends, family, and others, and by engaging in self-care and positive relationships, you can achieve optimal living for mind, body, and soul.

14: Physical Health for Optimal Living

Physical health plays a significant role in achieving optimal living and true happiness. Good physical health helps to increase energy levels, improve mood, and reduce the risk of chronic diseases. In this chapter, we will discuss the importance of physical health for optimal living and provide practical tips for improving physical health.

Why is Physical Health Important for Optimal Living?

Physical health is important for optimal living because it:

– Increases energy levels and reduces fatigue

– Improves mood and overall sense of well-being

– Reduces the risk of chronic diseases, such as heart disease, diabetes, and certain types of cancer

– Improves sleep quality and duration

– Enhances the ability to engage in physical activities and hobbies

How to Improve Physical Health for Optimal Living

14: PHYSICAL HEALTH FOR OPTIMAL LIVING

Improving physical health for optimal living requires a combination of lifestyle changes and self-care practices. Here are some practical tips for improving physical health:

– Eat a balanced diet: Consume a balanced diet that includes a variety of fruits, vegetables, whole grains, and lean proteins. Avoid processed foods, sugary drinks, and excessive amounts of caffeine and alcohol.

– Exercise regularly: Engage in regular physical activity, such as walking, running, cycling, or weightlifting. Aim for at least 30 minutes of moderate-intensity exercise, five days per week.

– Manage stress: Practice stress management techniques, such as mindfulness, meditation, or exercise, to reduce the negative impact of stress on physical health.

– Get adequate sleep: Aim for seven to eight hours of sleep per night to promote physical and mental well-being.

– Avoid harmful substances: Avoid tobacco, drugs, and excessive alcohol consumption, as these substances can have a negative impact on physical health.

– Visit the doctor regularly: Visit the doctor regularly for check-ups, preventive care, and to receive treatment for any physical health conditions.

– Practice self-care: Engage in self-care practices, such as stretching, yoga, or taking relaxing baths, to help maintain physical health and well-being.

In conclusion, physical health is critical for optimal living and true happiness. By making lifestyle changes and practicing self-care, you can improve your physical health and achieve optimal living for mind, body, and soul.

15: The Importance of Sleep for Optimal Living

Sleep is essential for physical, mental, and emotional well-being. It plays a critical role in supporting optimal living and true happiness. In this chapter, we will discuss the importance of sleep for optimal living and provide practical tips for improving sleep quality and duration.

Why is Sleep Important for Optimal Living?

Sleep is important for optimal living because it:

– Supports physical health by allowing the body to recover and repair from daily physical activity

– Improves cognitive function, including memory, attention, and decision-making

– Enhances mood and overall sense of well-being

– Supports the immune system and reduces the risk of chronic diseases

– Increases energy levels and reduces fatigue

How to Improve Sleep for Optimal Living

15: THE IMPORTANCE OF SLEEP FOR OPTIMAL LIVING

Improving sleep for optimal living requires a combination of lifestyle changes and self-care practices. Here are some practical tips for improving sleep quality and duration:

– Establish a sleep schedule: Create a consistent sleep schedule, going to bed and waking up at the same time every day, even on weekends.

– Create a sleep-friendly environment: Ensure that the sleeping environment is dark, quiet, cool, and comfortable.

– Avoid caffeine, alcohol, and nicotine: Avoid consuming caffeine, alcohol, and nicotine, especially in the hours leading up to bedtime, as they can interfere with sleep quality.

– Limit screen time: Reduce the amount of time spent using electronic devices, such as smartphones and laptops, before bedtime, as the blue light emitted by these devices can interfere with sleep.

– Engage in physical activity: Engage in regular physical activity, such as walking, running, cycling, or weightlifting, during the day, as physical activity can improve sleep quality and duration.

– Practice relaxation techniques: Engage in relaxation techniques, such as mindfulness, meditation, or yoga, to reduce stress and promote relaxation before bedtime.

– Seek help if necessary: If sleep problems persist, seek help from a medical professional.

In conclusion, sleep is critical for optimal living and true happiness. By making lifestyle changes and practicing self-care, you can improve your sleep quality and duration and achieve optimal living for mind, body, and soul.

16: Nutrition for Optimal Living

Good nutrition is essential for physical, mental, and emotional well-being. Eating a balanced diet that includes a variety of nutrient-rich foods can help support optimal living and true happiness. In this chapter, we will discuss the importance of nutrition for optimal living and provide practical tips for making healthy food choices.

Why is Nutrition Important for Optimal Living?

Nutrition is important for optimal living because it:

– Supports physical health by providing the body with the necessary nutrients to function properly

– Improves cognitive function, including memory, attention, and decision-making

– Enhances mood and overall sense of well-being

– Supports the immune system and reduces the risk of chronic diseases

– Provides energy to support physical activity and daily life

How to Improve Nutrition for Optimal Living

Improving nutrition for optimal living requires making healthier food choices and understanding the importance of portion control. Here are some practical tips for making healthy food choices:

– Eat a variety of foods: Include a variety of nutrient-rich foods, such as fruits, vegetables, whole grains, lean proteins, and healthy fats, in your diet.

– Limit processed foods: Limit the consumption of processed foods, such as junk food and fast food, which are high in sugar, salt, and unhealthy fats.

– Eat breakfast: Start the day with a healthy breakfast, such as oatmeal with fruit and nuts or eggs with whole grain toast, to provide energy and support mental clarity.

– Stay hydrated: Drink plenty of water throughout the day to stay hydrated and support physical function.

– Control portion sizes: Be mindful of portion sizes when eating, as overeating can lead to weight gain and other health problems.

– Plan ahead: Plan and prepare healthy meals and snacks in

advance to make healthy food choices easier.

− Seek help if necessary: If you need help improving your nutrition, seek help from a dietitian or nutritionist.

In conclusion, good nutrition is critical for optimal living and true happiness. By making healthier food choices and understanding the importance of portion control, you can support optimal living for mind, body, and soul.

17: Exercise for Optimal Living

Introduction:

Exercise is a critical aspect of optimal living as it not only keeps the body healthy but also benefits the mind and soul. Regular physical activity helps to maintain a healthy weight, reduces the risk of chronic diseases, and improves mental health. In this chapter, we will explore the various types of exercises and their benefits, as well as tips for making exercise a regular part of your life.

Benefits of Exercise:

Physical activity is essential for overall health and well-being. Regular exercise can help you:

– Maintain a healthy weight and reduce the risk of obesity

– Improve cardiovascular health and reduce the risk of heart disease

– Strengthen bones and muscles, reducing the risk of osteoporosis and injury

– Improve mental health and reduce the risk of depression and anxiety

– Boost energy levels and increase overall physical fitness

Types of Exercise:

There are many different types of exercise, each with its unique benefits. Some popular types of exercise include:

– Aerobic Exercise: This type of exercise involves continuous and rhythmic movements that raise the heart rate and improve cardiovascular health. Examples of aerobic exercise include running, cycling, and swimming.

– Strength Training: This type of exercise focuses on building muscle strength and endurance. It can be performed with weights, resistance bands, or bodyweight exercises.

– Yoga and Pilates: These forms of exercise combine physical movements with breathing and meditation techniques to improve flexibility, strength, and mental health.

– HIIT (High-Intensity Interval Training): This type of exercise involves short, intense bursts of activity followed by periods of rest. HIIT is an efficient and effective way to improve cardiovascular health and burn calories.

Making Exercise a Regular Part of Your Life:

– Set Realistic Goals: Start by setting achievable goals that fit into your lifestyle. It can be as simple as a 30-minute walk each day or three strength training sessions per week.

– Find an Activity You Enjoy: Choose an exercise that you enjoy, as this will make it easier to stick to a regular routine. If you don't enjoy running, for example, try cycling or swimming instead.

– Make it a Priority: Treat exercise as a priority, just like you would any other important commitment in your life. Schedule your workouts at a time that works best for you, and make it a non-negotiable part of your routine.

– Find a Workout Buddy: Having a workout partner can be a great motivator and help keep you accountable. Find someone who shares your fitness goals and schedule workouts together.

– Mix it Up: To avoid boredom and prevent injury, vary your exercise routine by trying new activities and switching up your routine regularly.

Conclusion:

17: EXERCISE FOR OPTIMAL LIVING

Exercise is a vital component of optimal living and provides numerous physical and mental health benefits. By making exercise a regular part of your routine, you can improve your overall health, reduce the risk of chronic diseases, and increase your overall happiness and well-being. Whether you prefer aerobics, strength training, yoga, or any other form of physical activity, find an exercise that you enjoy and make it a priority in your life.

18: Managing Chronic Illness for Optimal Living

Introduction

Chronic illness can be a challenging aspect of life, affecting both physical and emotional well-being. It is a long-term medical condition that can interfere with daily activities, relationships, and overall quality of life. Despite this, it is possible to manage chronic illness and maintain optimal living. In this chapter, we will discuss how to manage chronic illness and how to make the necessary changes to lead a fulfilling life.

Understand the Chronic Illness

The first step in managing chronic illness is to understand it. It is essential to be informed about the specific condition, including its symptoms, causes, and treatments. This knowledge can help you to take control of your illness and make informed decisions about your health. You can also seek advice from healthcare professionals who can provide you with the most current information on your specific condition.

18: MANAGING CHRONIC ILLNESS FOR OPTIMAL LIVING

Develop a Plan of Action

Once you have a clear understanding of your chronic illness, it is time to develop a plan of action. This plan should include self-care strategies, support from healthcare professionals, and lifestyle modifications. It is important to understand that managing chronic illness is a continuous process and requires patience, commitment, and persistence.

Self-Care Strategies

Self-care is a critical aspect of managing chronic illness. It includes taking care of your physical and emotional health, maintaining a healthy diet, and getting enough sleep. It is also essential to engage in activities that bring you joy and reduce stress, such as exercise, hobbies, and spending time with loved ones.

Working with Healthcare Professionals

Healthcare professionals can provide you with essential support in managing chronic illness. They can help you to develop a care plan, monitor your condition, and provide treatment options. It is essential to establish open and honest communication with your healthcare team to ensure that they have a clear understanding of your needs and concerns.

Lifestyle Modifications

Lifestyle modifications are an essential aspect of managing chronic illness. This may include changes to your diet, exercise, and sleeping habits. It may also require limiting or avoiding exposure to environmental triggers that can worsen your condition.

Building a Support System

Managing chronic illness can be challenging, and it is essential to have a support system. This may include family members, friends, or support groups specifically for individuals with the same chronic illness. A support system can provide you with emotional support, encouragement, and a sense of community.

Conclusion

Chronic illness can be challenging, but it is possible to manage it and lead a fulfilling life. By understanding your illness, developing a plan of action, engaging in self-care, working with healthcare professionals, making lifestyle modifications, and building a support system, you can manage your chronic illness and achieve optimal living. Remember to be patient, persistent, and stay positive, as this will help you to navigate the ups and downs of managing chronic illness and maintain a high quality of life.

19: Mental Health for Optimal Living

Mental health is an integral part of overall health and well-being, and it plays a significant role in how we experience and navigate our daily lives. In this chapter, we will discuss the importance of mental health for optimal living and provide practical tips and techniques for improving and maintaining good mental health.

First, let's define what we mean by mental health. Mental health refers to a person's emotional, psychological, and social well-being. It involves a person's ability to cope with the normal stresses of life, work productively, and make meaningful contributions to their community. Mental health is not just the absence of mental illness, but it is a state of well-being that allows individuals to enjoy life and engage in meaningful activities.

It is important to note that mental health is not a static state and can change over time, depending on a variety of factors such as life events, stress levels, and overall health. That's why it is important to regularly monitor and care for your mental health.

So, how can you improve and maintain good mental health? Here are some tips and techniques that can help:

– Practice self-care: Self-care is a critical component of mental health. It involves taking care of your physical, emotional, and mental well-being, and it can help to reduce stress, increase resilience, and improve overall mental health. Self-care can include activities such as exercise, healthy eating, meditation, and spending time with friends and family.

– Connect with others: Building positive relationships with friends, family, and community can help to improve mental health and provide a supportive network during difficult times.

– Engage in meaningful activities: Engaging in activities that bring joy and fulfillment can help to improve mental health and overall well-being. This can include hobbies, volunteer work, or pursuing personal interests.

– Manage stress: Stress is a normal part of life, but if it becomes chronic, it can have negative effects on mental health. It is important to identify the sources of stress and find healthy ways to manage it, such as through exercise, mindfulness, or seeking support from friends and family.

– Get enough sleep: Sleep is essential for overall health, including mental health. Lack of sleep can lead to increased stress, decreased cognitive functioning, and impaired mood. It is recommended to aim for 7-9 hours of sleep each night.

– Seek professional help if needed: If you are experiencing symptoms of a mental health disorder, such as anxiety, depression, or post-traumatic stress disorder (PTSD), it is important to seek help from a mental health professional. They can provide a diagnosis, treatment options, and support to help manage symptoms.

It is important to remember that mental health is a continuous process, and it is essential to engage in regular self-care and seek support when needed. By prioritizing mental health and incorporating healthy habits into your daily routine, you can improve your overall well-being and achieve optimal living.

In conclusion, mental health is a critical component of overall health and well-being, and it is essential to prioritize and care for it. By practicing self-care, connecting with others, engaging in meaningful activities, managing stress, getting enough sleep, and seeking professional help when needed, you can improve your mental health and achieve optimal living.

20: Overcoming Anxiety for Optimal Living

Introduction:

Anxiety is a normal and often healthy emotion. However, when a person regularly feels disproportionate levels of anxiety, it can become a debilitating condition that interferes with daily activities. Overcoming anxiety requires a combination of self-awareness, self-care, and, in some cases, professional help. This chapter provides an overview of the different types of anxiety, their causes, and strategies for managing and overcoming them.

Types of Anxiety Disorders:

There are several types of anxiety disorders, each with their own symptoms and causes. The most common include:

– Generalized Anxiety Disorder (GAD) - This is characterized by excessive, unrealistic worry and tension, even when there is little or no cause for concern.

– Panic Disorder - This type of anxiety is characterized by sudden, intense fear and discomfort that may feel like a heart attack or other life-threatening event.

– Social Anxiety Disorder (SAD) - This type of anxiety is characterized by intense fear or embarrassment in social situations.

– Specific Phobias - This type of anxiety is characterized by intense fear or avoidance of specific objects or situations, such as flying or public speaking.

– Obsessive-Compulsive Disorder (OCD) - This type of anxiety is characterized by repetitive, intrusive thoughts (obsessions) and behaviors (compulsions) that the person feels compelled to perform.

Understanding the Causes of Anxiety:

Anxiety can be caused by a variety of factors, including:

– Genetics - Anxiety can run in families and may be influenced by certain genes.

– Life experiences - Traumatic events, such as abuse or neglect, can increase a person's risk of developing anxiety.

– Brain chemistry - Imbalances in brain chemicals, such as neurotransmitters, can play a role in the development of anxiety.

– Substance abuse - Substance abuse, such as alcohol or drug use, can increase anxiety symptoms.

– Medical conditions - Medical conditions, such as heart disease or thyroid problems, can also increase anxiety symptoms.

Managing and Overcoming Anxiety:

There are several effective strategies for managing and overcoming anxiety, including:

– Cognitive-behavioral therapy (CBT) - This type of therapy focuses on changing negative thought patterns and behaviors associated with anxiety.

– Exposure therapy - This type of therapy involves gradually exposing a person to the object or situation they fear in a controlled environment to help them overcome their fear.

– Mindfulness and meditation - Practicing mindfulness and meditation can help to calm the mind and reduce anxiety symptoms.

– Exercise - Regular exercise can help to reduce stress and anxiety and improve overall mental health.

– Medication - In some cases, medication, such as anti-anxiety drugs or antidepressants, may be prescribed to help manage anxiety symptoms.

– Lifestyle changes - Making healthy lifestyle changes, such as getting enough sleep, eating a nutritious diet, and limiting alcohol and caffeine consumption, can also help to reduce anxiety symptoms.

Conclusion:

Anxiety is a common and often debilitating condition that can interfere with daily activities. However, with the right combination of self-care, therapy, and medication, it is possible to overcome anxiety and achieve optimal living. By learning to manage and control anxiety symptoms, you can regain control of your life and experience true happiness and fulfillment.

21: Overcoming Depression for Optimal Living

Depression is a common mental health condition that affects millions of people worldwide. It can have a profound impact on your life, causing feelings of sadness, hopelessness, and a lack of energy or motivation. However, despite how overwhelming depression can feel, it is a treatable condition and it is possible to overcome it and achieve optimal living.

In this chapter, we will explore the causes of depression, common symptoms, and effective strategies for managing and overcoming depression. By taking a proactive approach to your mental health, you can learn to live a happier, more fulfilling life.

Understanding the Causes of Depression

Depression is a complex condition that can be caused by a combination of genetic, biological, environmental, and psychological factors. Some of the most common causes of depression include:

– Genetics: Depression can run in families, and research

suggests that certain genes may increase a person's risk of developing the condition.

– Brain chemistry: Imbalances in neurotransmitters, the chemicals in the brain that regulate mood, can lead to depression.

– Life events: Traumatic or stressful life events, such as the death of a loved one, relationship problems, financial difficulties, or job loss, can trigger depression.

– Chronic illness: People with chronic physical health conditions, such as diabetes, heart disease, or cancer, are more likely to experience depression.

Common Symptoms of Depression

Depression can manifest in a number of ways, and the symptoms can vary from person to person. Some common symptoms of depression include:

– Feelings of sadness, hopelessness, or emptiness

– Loss of interest in activities that were once enjoyable

– Changes in appetite and sleep patterns

– Fatigue and low energy

– Difficulty concentrating and making decisions

– Thoughts of self-harm or suicide

If you are experiencing any of these symptoms, it is important to seek professional help. A mental health professional can diagnose depression and develop an effective treatment plan that is right for you.

Strategies for Overcoming Depression

There are a variety of effective strategies for managing and overcoming depression. Here are a few of the most effective:

– Therapy: Talking to a mental health professional, such as a therapist or psychologist, can help you gain insight into your thoughts and feelings, and provide you with coping strategies to manage depression.

– Antidepressant medication: Antidepressants can help to balance the neurotransmitters in the brain that regulate mood, and relieve symptoms of depression.

– Exercise: Exercise has been shown to have a positive effect on mood, and can help to relieve symptoms of depression.

– Mindfulness and meditation: Mindfulness and meditation practices can help to calm the mind, reduce stress, and improve mood.

– Healthy lifestyle habits: Eating a nutritious diet, getting adequate sleep, and engaging in regular physical activity can help to improve mood and promote overall health and well-being.

– Support from others: Surrounding yourself with supportive friends and family members, or participating in a support group, can help to provide emotional support and encouragement as you work through your depression.

Building a Support System for Optimal Living

Having a strong support system is an important part of overcoming depression and achieving optimal living. Whether it's a friend, family member, therapist, or support group, having people in your life who care about you and support you can make a huge difference.

21: OVERCOMING DEPRESSION FOR OPTIMAL LIVING

If you are struggling with depression, it is important to reach out for help. This can be as simple as talking to a trusted friend or family member, or seeking professional help from a mental health professional. You do not have to face depression

22: Coping with Trauma for Optimal Living

Trauma can take many forms, including physical, emotional, sexual, or psychological abuse, accidents, natural disasters, or war. Regardless of the cause, trauma can have a lasting impact on a person's mental and emotional well-being. It can leave individuals feeling overwhelmed, anxious, and depressed. However, with the right support, individuals can learn how to cope with trauma and reclaim their lives.

The first step in overcoming trauma is to recognize and acknowledge what has happened. Many people try to ignore their traumatic experiences or push them to the back of their minds, but this can actually make the symptoms worse. Acknowledge your feelings and allow yourself to experience them, even if they are uncomfortable.

Next, it is important to seek professional help from a therapist or counselor. A mental health professional can provide you with the support and guidance you need to work through your traumatic experiences and develop healthy coping mechanisms. They can also help you understand the impact that trauma has had on your life and provide you with strategies for managing your symptoms.

It is also important to take care of your physical health. This can include eating a healthy diet, getting regular exercise, and getting enough sleep. Taking care of your body can help you feel better mentally and emotionally, and it can also help you manage the symptoms of trauma.

In addition, it can be helpful to engage in mindfulness practices, such as meditation or yoga, which can help you stay in the present moment and reduce stress and anxiety. Engaging in physical activities, such as exercise or hobbies, can also be helpful in managing symptoms and promoting mental wellness.

Finally, it is important to build a strong support system. This can include friends, family, support groups, or a trusted therapist. Having people in your life who understand what you are going through and can provide you with emotional support can be incredibly helpful in overcoming trauma.

In conclusion, coping with trauma can be a challenging process, but with the right support and strategies, individuals can learn to manage their symptoms and reclaim their lives.

22: COPING WITH TRAUMA FOR OPTIMAL LIVING

By seeking professional help, taking care of your physical health, engaging in mindfulness practices, and building a strong support system, individuals can find hope and healing. Remember, you are not alone, and help is available.

23: Building Emotional Intelligence for Optimal Living

Emotional intelligence is the ability to recognize, understand, and manage our own emotions, as well as the emotions of others. It involves a set of skills that help us to navigate our relationships with others and make informed decisions. Building emotional intelligence is an important aspect of optimal living, as it can significantly enhance our overall well-being and happiness. In this chapter, we will explore the importance of emotional intelligence and discuss how to develop this critical skill.

The Importance of Emotional Intelligence

Emotional intelligence has been shown to play a crucial role in our personal and professional lives. Research has indicated that individuals with high levels of emotional intelligence tend to experience more success in their careers, stronger relationships, and greater overall life satisfaction. For example, individuals with high emotional intelligence are often able to manage stress better, communicate more effectively, and resolve conflicts in a more positive manner. Additionally, individuals with strong emotional intelligence tend to be more resilient in the face of adversity, as they are better able to cope with and overcome life's challenges.

Developing Emotional Intelligence

Developing emotional intelligence is a lifelong process, but it is never too late to start. There are several key steps that can help us build our emotional intelligence and improve our overall well-being:

– Awareness of your emotions: The first step in building emotional intelligence is becoming aware of our own emotions. This requires us to pause and reflect on how we are feeling in any given moment. It also requires us to identify the triggers that cause our emotions and to understand the impact that our emotions have on our behavior and thoughts.

– Empathy: Empathy involves the ability to understand and share the feelings of others. To develop empathy, try to put yourself in other people's shoes, and imagine how they might be feeling. This can help you to better understand their perspective and to respond in a more compassionate and understanding manner.

23: BUILDING EMOTIONAL INTELLIGENCE FOR OP-
TIMAL LIVING

– Regulation of emotions: Emotional regulation involves managing our emotions so that they don't get the best of us. This requires us to understand our own triggers and to develop strategies for managing our emotions. For example, we can take deep breaths, go for a walk, or practice mindfulness to help us regulate our emotions.

– Communication skills: Effective communication is a critical aspect of emotional intelligence. This involves being able to express our feelings in a clear and concise manner, as well as actively listening to others and considering their perspectives.

– Practice self-compassion: Self-compassion involves treating ourselves with kindness, care, and understanding, even in difficult moments. When we practice self-compassion, we are less likely to be critical of ourselves and more likely to develop a positive and supportive internal dialogue.

– Seek support: Building emotional intelligence is a challenging process, and it is important to seek support from others when needed. This could involve talking to a trusted friend, family member, or therapist. Additionally, consider seeking out training or workshops that focus on building emotional intelligence.

In conclusion, building emotional intelligence is an important aspect of optimal living. By developing this critical skill,
we can enhance our relationships, improve our overall well-
being, and achieve greater happiness and success in our
personal and professional lives. As with any new skill, building emotional intelligence takes time, effort, and practice.
However, the benefits of doing so are well worth the investment.

24: Building a Growth Mindset for Optimal Living

In the pursuit of optimal living, it is crucial to cultivate a growth mindset. This type of mindset involves the belief that one's abilities, talents, and intelligence can be developed through effort and perseverance. By embracing a growth mindset, individuals can overcome obstacles, reach their full potential, and achieve true happiness.

The opposite of a growth mindset is a fixed mindset. Individuals with a fixed mindset believe that their abilities, talents, and intelligence are set in stone and cannot be changed. They often shy away from challenges and may avoid taking risks or trying new things out of fear of failure.

One of the key benefits of a growth mindset is increased resilience. People with a growth mindset are better equipped to handle setbacks and failures because they believe that they can learn and grow from their experiences. They are more likely to approach challenges with determination and a willingness to try again, which can lead to increased self-confidence and success over time.

Another benefit of a growth mindset is increased creativity

and innovation. People with a growth mindset are more likely to take risks and try new things, which can lead to breakthroughs and creative solutions. They are also more likely to seek out feedback and use it to improve, rather than becoming defensive or taking it as a personal attack.

To develop a growth mindset, it is important to focus on effort and perseverance, rather than just the end result. When faced with a challenge, it is helpful to approach it with a willingness to learn and grow, rather than simply giving up when faced with obstacles. It is also important to embrace failure as a natural part of the learning process, rather than viewing it as a personal failure or proof of one's inability to succeed.

One way to develop a growth mindset is by seeking out challenges and new experiences. This can include taking on a new hobby, learning a new skill, or volunteering for a new role at work. By stepping outside of one's comfort zone, individuals can develop their abilities and increase their confidence in their ability to succeed.

It is also helpful to seek out feedback from others and to actively seek out opportunities for growth and self-improvement. This can include attending workshops or conferences, seeking out mentorship or coaching, or taking online courses.

Finally, it is important to cultivate a positive and growth-oriented mindset by focusing on one's strengths and abilities, rather than dwelling on weaknesses or setbacks. Surrounding oneself with positive, supportive people and engaging in activities that bring joy and fulfillment can also help to build a growth mindset.

In conclusion, building a growth mindset is a crucial aspect of optimal living. By embracing a belief in the ability to grow and improve, individuals can overcome obstacles, reach their full potential, and achieve true happiness. With a focus on effort, perseverance, and a positive outlook, anyone can cultivate a growth mindset and reap the benefits of increased resilience, creativity, and success.

25: Building a Strong Work Ethic for Optimal Living

Introduction:

In today's fast-paced world, success and happiness are highly coveted commodities. However, they can often be elusive and difficult to attain. One of the keys to achieving these desirable outcomes is having a strong work ethic. In this chapter, we will explore what work ethic means, why it's important, and how to cultivate one for optimal living.

What is a Strong Work Ethic?

A strong work ethic is a set of moral principles and values that guide an individual's behavior and work habits. It is a commitment to excellence, diligence, and persistence in the pursuit of one's goals and responsibilities. A person with a strong work ethic is known for their integrity, reliability, and dedication to their work. They take pride in their achievements and take responsibility for their actions, both in and outside of the workplace.

Why is a Strong Work Ethic Important?

Having a strong work ethic can bring numerous benefits to

your life. It can improve your overall quality of life, help you reach your goals, and lead to increased success and satisfaction in both your personal and professional life. Here are some of the key benefits of having a strong work ethic:

– Improved Self-Esteem: When you have a strong work ethic, you are more likely to feel proud of your accomplishments and be confident in your abilities. This improved self-esteem can translate into greater happiness and well-being.

– Increased Success: People with a strong work ethic are more likely to be successful in their careers and personal endeavors. This is because they are more likely to put in the effort and work necessary to achieve their goals.

– Better Relationships: Having a strong work ethic can also improve your relationships. People will respect you more when they see your dedication and integrity in the way you approach your work and responsibilities.

– Improved Quality of Life: A strong work ethic can help improve your quality of life by reducing stress and increasing your sense of fulfillment. When you are dedicated and hard-working, you are more likely to feel a sense of purpose and satisfaction in your life.

How to Cultivate a Strong Work Ethic

Developing a strong work ethic is not something that happens overnight. It takes time, effort, and dedication. Here are some steps you can take to cultivate a strong work ethic:

– Set Goals: Setting goals is the first step in developing a strong work ethic. Without goals, it can be difficult to know what you are working towards and what you need to do to get there. Start by setting realistic, achievable goals for yourself and then create a plan to achieve them.

– Prioritize: Once you have set your goals, it's important to prioritize your work and responsibilities. Make a list of the most important tasks you need to complete and then focus on completing them before moving on to less important tasks.

– Stay Focused: When you are working, it's important to stay focused on your tasks. Avoid distractions and try to eliminate any obstacles that may be preventing you from getting your work done.

25: BUILDING A STRONG WORK ETHIC FOR OPTIMAL LIVING

– Practice Discipline: Discipline is an important part of having a strong work ethic. It means following through on your commitments and responsibilities, even when it's difficult or not convenient. Make a habit of doing what you need to do, even when you don't feel like it.

– Be Reliable: People with a strong work ethic are known for their reliability. They do what they say they will do and are there when they are needed. Make sure you are dependable and follow through on your commitments, both in and outside of the workplace.

26: Finding Work-Life Balance for Optimal Living

Introduction

In today's fast-paced and highly competitive world, finding the right balance between work and personal life can be a challenging task. The constant pressure to meet deadlines, perform well, and achieve success in the workplace can often lead to neglecting other important aspects of life such as family, relationships, and personal well-being. This can lead to feelings of burnout, stress, and unhappiness, affecting both our professional and personal life.

However, by finding the right balance between work and life, individuals can not only lead a more fulfilling life but also perform better in the workplace. This chapter will provide a comprehensive guide to help you find the right balance between work and life for optimal living.

The Importance of Work-Life Balance

Achieving work-life balance is crucial for leading a happy, healthy, and fulfilling life. When work and personal life are in balance, individuals experience a sense of control over their lives and are able to prioritize their time and energy effectively. This can lead to reduced stress levels, improved mental health, and enhanced overall well-being.

Moreover, individuals who are able to achieve work-life balance are also more productive and efficient in the workplace. They are able to bring their best selves to work, concentrate better, and make more informed decisions. This can lead to increased job satisfaction and better performance, leading to greater success in the workplace.

Tips for Achieving Work-Life Balance

– Set Priorities

One of the first steps towards finding work-life balance is to set priorities. Make a list of the things that are important to you and prioritize them based on their level of significance. This will help you allocate your time and energy effectively, ensuring that you are spending time on the things that matter most to you.

– Set Boundaries

Setting boundaries between work and personal life is key to

achieving work-life balance. This means not checking work emails or taking work calls outside of work hours, setting aside dedicated time for personal pursuits and relationships, and not allowing work to interfere with personal time. By setting these boundaries, individuals can prevent work from taking over their lives and ensure that they have adequate time for rest and relaxation.

– Practice Time Management

Effective time management is critical to achieving work-life balance. This involves scheduling time for work tasks, personal pursuits, and rest and relaxation, and ensuring that you stick to the schedule. By managing your time effectively, you can ensure that you have adequate time for both work and personal life, and prevent work from taking over your life.

– Stay Active and Engaged

Physical activity is an essential component of work-life balance. Regular exercise can help reduce stress levels, improve mental health, and enhance overall well-being. It is also important to stay engaged in hobbies and interests outside of work, as this can help individuals maintain a healthy work-life balance by providing a sense of purpose and fulfillment outside of the workplace.

– Maintain a Positive Attitude

Maintaining a positive attitude is key to achieving work-life balance. This means adopting a growth mindset, being proactive, and focusing on solutions rather than problems. By maintaining a positive attitude, individuals can approach challenges with a sense of purpose and determination, and be better equipped to find a healthy balance between work and life.

Conclusion

In conclusion, finding the right balance between work and life is crucial for leading a happy, healthy, and fulfilling life. By setting priorities, setting boundaries, practicing time management, staying active and engaged, and maintaining a positive attitude, individuals can achieve work-life balance and lead an optimal life.

Remember, work-life balance is a journey and it is import-

ant to be flexible and adapt to changes as they arise. Be patient with yourself and don't be afraid to make changes as
needed. The most important thing is to find what works for
you and stick to it.

Finally, it is essential to make self-care a priority in your
quest for work-life balance. This means taking care of your
physical and mental health, getting enough sleep, and engaging in activities that bring you joy and happiness. By putting yourself first, you can create the foundation for a life
that is fulfilling and in balance.

In this comprehensive guide to optimal living, we hope that
the information provided in this chapter will help you find
the right balance between work and life, and achieve true
happiness in both your professional and personal life.

27: Building a Strong Financial Foundation for Optimal Living

Introduction

Financial stability and security is an essential component of optimal living. Money can be a major source of stress and anxiety, but with proper planning and management, individuals can build a strong financial foundation that will allow them to lead a life of financial freedom and peace of mind. This chapter will provide a comprehensive guide to help you build a strong financial foundation for optimal living.

The Importance of Financial Planning

Financial planning is a critical component of optimal living. It involves setting financial goals, developing a budget, and creating a plan to achieve those goals. By taking control of your finances, individuals can ensure that they have the resources they need to lead a comfortable and fulfilling life, now and in the future.

Moreover, financial planning also helps individuals make informed decisions about spending, saving, and investing, which can lead to greater financial stability and security. This can reduce stress levels and improve overall well-being, as individuals have a sense of control over their finances and are better equipped to handle financial challenges.

Tips for Building a Strong Financial Foundation

– Set Financial Goals

The first step towards building a strong financial foundation is to set financial goals. This involves determining what you want to achieve in the short-term, medium-term, and long-term, and setting achievable and realistic goals for each time frame. This will provide a roadmap for your financial planning and help you prioritize your spending and saving.

– Develop a Budget

Developing a budget is an essential component of financial planning. This involves tracking your income and expenses, determining your spending habits, and creating a plan to manage your money effectively. By creating a budget, individuals can ensure that they have the resources they need to meet their financial goals, and can make informed decisions about spending, saving, and investing.

– Reduce Debt

Reducing debt is a critical component of building a strong financial foundation. This involves paying off high-interest debt, such as credit card balances, and consolidating loans to lower your monthly payments. By reducing debt, individuals can free up more of their monthly income for saving and investing, and improve their overall financial stability.

– Save and Invest

Saving and investing is an important component of building a strong financial foundation. This involves setting aside a portion of your income each month for savings, investing in a diverse portfolio of assets, and taking advantage of employer-sponsored retirement plans, such as 401(k)s, to ensure that you have adequate resources for the future. By saving and investing, individuals can build wealth, reduce financial stress, and ensure that they have the resources they need for a comfortable retirement.

27: BUILDING A STRONG FINANCIAL FOUNDATION FOR OPTIMAL LIVING

– Seek Professional Advice

Finally, seeking professional advice is an important component of building a strong financial foundation. This involves working with a financial advisor to develop a customized plan that takes into account your unique circumstances and goals. By seeking professional advice, individuals can gain access to expert knowledge and guidance, and be better equipped to make informed decisions about their finances.

Conclusion

In conclusion, building a strong financial foundation is an essential component of optimal living. By setting financial goals, developing a budget, reducing debt, saving and investing, and seeking professional advice, individuals can achieve financial freedom and peace of mind.

Remember, financial planning is a journey, and it is important to be patient and consistent in your efforts. It may take time to see results, but by following these tips and taking control of your finances, you can build a strong financial foundation that will allow you to lead a life of financial stability and security.

27: BUILDING A STRONG FINANCIAL FOUNDATION
FOR OPTIMAL LIVING

In this comprehensive guide to optimal living, we hope that the information provided in this chapter will help you build a strong financial foundation, and empower you to make informed decisions about your finances. By taking control of your finances, you can create the foundation for a life of financial freedom and peace of mind, and achieve true happiness in both your personal and financial life.

Remember, financial planning is not just about managing your money, it's about managing your life. By taking a holistic approach to your finances, you can create a future that is bright, secure, and full of possibilities. So start today, and take the first step towards building a strong financial foundation for optimal living.

28: Creating a Happy Home for Optimal Living

Introduction

The home is where individuals spend the majority of their time, and it should be a place that promotes happiness, comfort, and well-being. A happy home can provide a safe and secure environment that allows individuals to relax, recharge, and pursue their passions and interests. This chapter will provide a comprehensive guide to help you create a happy home for optimal living.

The Importance of a Happy Home

A happy home is essential to optimal living. It provides a sanctuary from the stress and chaos of daily life, and creates a positive and supportive environment that promotes happiness, well-being, and personal growth. A happy home can also improve relationships with family and friends, and create a sense of community and belonging.

In addition, a happy home can have a positive impact on mental health, as individuals have a safe and comfortable environment where they can escape from the stress and pressures of daily life. Furthermore, a happy home can also improve physical health, as individuals are more likely to engage in activities such as exercise, healthy eating, and self-care when they have a positive and supportive environment.

Tips for Creating a Happy Home

– Personalize Your Space

The first step towards creating a happy home is to personalize your space. This involves incorporating items, colors, and textures that reflect your personal style and interests, and creating an environment that is uniquely yours. Personalizing your space can make your home feel more welcoming and comfortable, and improve your overall sense of well-being.

– Create a Relaxing Environment

Creating a relaxing environment is an important component of a happy home. This involves incorporating elements such as comfortable furniture, soft lighting, and calming colors to create a peaceful and inviting space. By creating a relaxing environment, individuals can reduce stress levels, and create a space where they can recharge and unwind.

– Foster Positive Relationships

Fostering positive relationships is an important component of a happy home. This involves creating an environment that promotes communication, cooperation, and mutual respect among family and friends. This can include regular family dinners, game nights, and other activities that promote positive interactions and strengthen relationships.

– Encourage Personal Growth and Wellness

Encouraging personal growth and wellness is an important component of a happy home. This involves creating a space where individuals can pursue their passions and interests, engage in physical activity, and practice self-care. This can include setting up a home gym, creating a home office or workspace, and incorporating elements such as plants, books, and other items that promote growth and well-being.

– Keep Your Home Clean and Organized

Finally, keeping your home clean and organized is an important component of a happy home. This involves developing habits such as regularly cleaning and decluttering, and creating an organized system for storing items. By keeping your home clean and organized, individuals can reduce stress levels, improve their mental clarity, and create a space that is both beautiful and functional.

Conclusion

In conclusion, creating a happy home is an essential component of optimal living. By personalizing your space, creating a relaxing environment, fostering positive relationships, encouraging personal growth and wellness, and keeping your home clean and organized, individuals can create a safe and secure environment that promotes happiness and well-being.

Remember, your home should be a reflection of who you are and what you value. By taking the time to create a happy home, you can create a space that supports your personal and professional goals, and allows you to thrive in both your personal and professional life.

A happy home can provide a foundation for a rich and fulfilling life, and can be the starting point for a journey of self-discovery and personal growth. By taking control of your home environment, you can create a space that inspires creativity, nurtures relationships, and supports your overall well-being.

In this comprehensive guide to optimal living, we hope that the information provided in this chapter will help you create a happy home, and empower you to take control of your living space. With these tips and strategies, you can turn your home into a place of peace, happiness, and comfort, and lay the foundation for a life of optimal living.

So, start today, and take the first step towards creating a happy home for optimal living. Remember, your home is a reflection of who you are, and it should be a place where you feel happy, relaxed, and fulfilled. With a little effort and dedication, you can create a home that supports your personal and professional goals, and promotes happiness and well-being in your life.

29: Building Strong Parenting Skills for Optimal Living

Building strong parenting skills is essential for creating a happy and fulfilling family life. As a parent, you play a vital role in shaping your child's future, and your actions and attitudes will have a lasting impact on their development. By focusing on your own growth and development as a parent, you can create a supportive and loving environment that encourages your children to thrive.

In this comprehensive guide to optimal living, we will explore the various aspects of parenting, and provide tips and strategies to help you become the best parent you can be. Whether you are a new parent or have years of experience, the information in this chapter will help you to refine your skills and deepen your understanding of what it takes to raise happy, healthy children.

One of the most important aspects of parenting is providing a consistent and supportive environment for your children. This means setting clear expectations and boundaries, and creating an atmosphere of trust and respect. Children need to feel safe and secure in order to thrive, and it is up to you as a parent to provide this environment.

29: BUILDING STRONG PARENTING SKILLS FOR OPTIMAL LIVING

Another important aspect of parenting is providing emotional support. Children need to know that they are loved and valued, and that their feelings matter. By listening to your children, expressing empathy and compassion, and validating their emotions, you can help them to develop strong self-esteem and resilience.

Effective communication is also an essential component of good parenting. By using active listening skills, expressing yourself clearly and calmly, and avoiding criticism and blame, you can foster positive relationships with your children and help them to understand and manage their emotions.

In addition to these basic principles, there are many other strategies and techniques that can help you to build strong parenting skills. From developing a positive attitude and staying calm in the face of challenges, to setting goals and making time for self-care, there are many steps you can take to become the best parent you can be.

So, whether you are just starting out on your parenting journey, or you are looking to deepen your skills and understanding, this chapter on building strong parenting skills for optimal living is here to help. With its comprehensive guide to parenting, you will have the tools you need to create a happy and fulfilling family life, and support your children as they grow and develop into confident and successful adults.

30: Building Strong Marriage and Relationships for Optimal Living

Building strong marriage and relationships is an essential part of achieving true happiness and optimal living. Whether you are single, dating, or in a committed relationship, the quality of your relationships has a profound impact on your overall well-being and happiness.

In this comprehensive guide to optimal living, we will explore the various aspects of building strong relationships, and provide tips and strategies to help you strengthen your connections with others and achieve greater happiness in your personal and professional life.

One of the keys to building strong relationships is effective communication. By developing your listening and speaking skills, and avoiding negative communication patterns like criticism and blame, you can foster positive and supportive relationships with those around you.

It is also important to have a positive attitude and approach to relationships. By focusing on the good in others, expressing gratitude and appreciation, and avoiding negative thoughts and behaviors, you can create a supportive and loving environment that promotes happiness and well-being.

In a committed relationship, such as marriage, it is also crucial to have shared values and goals. By working together towards common objectives, and supporting each other in your personal and professional growth, you can build a strong and fulfilling partnership that lasts a lifetime.

In addition to these basic principles, there are many other strategies and techniques that can help you to build strong relationships. From developing strong emotional intelligence and empathy, to making time for self-care and self-reflection, there are many steps you can take to achieve greater happiness in your relationships.

So, whether you are just starting out in your relationships, or you are looking to deepen and strengthen your existing connections, this chapter on building strong marriage and relationships for optimal living is here to help. With its comprehensive guide to relationship building, you will have the tools you need to create meaningful and fulfilling connections with others, and achieve greater happiness and well-being in your personal and professional life.

31: Building Strong Friendships for Optimal Living

Friendships are an essential component of a happy and fulfilling life. Having strong, supportive, and meaningful relationships with others can provide a sense of belonging, increase your overall happiness, and help you to navigate the ups and downs of life.

In this comprehensive guide to optimal living, we will explore the various aspects of building strong friendships, and provide tips and strategies to help you deepen your connections with others and achieve greater happiness in your personal and professional life.

One of the keys to building strong friendships is being a good listener. By actively listening to others and showing genuine interest in their lives, you can build a strong foundation of trust and support. Additionally, by being open and honest in your communication, and avoiding negative behaviors like criticism and blame, you can create a positive and supportive environment in your relationships.

Another important aspect of building strong friendships is finding common ground. Whether it's through shared interests, values, or goals, having common experiences and perspectives can deepen your connection with others and create a sense of closeness and understanding.

It is also essential to make time for your friendships. Whether it's through regular check-ins, spending time together, or simply staying in touch through social media and messaging, making time for your friends is essential for maintaining and strengthening your relationships.

In addition to these basic principles, there are many other strategies and techniques that can help you to build strong friendships. From developing your emotional intelligence and empathy, to participating in activities that bring people together, there are many ways to deepen your connections with others and achieve greater happiness in your personal and professional life.

So, whether you are just starting to build your social network, or you are looking to deepen and strengthen your existing relationships, this chapter on building strong friendships for optimal living is here to help. With its comprehensive guide to friendship building, you will have the tools you need to create meaningful and fulfilling connections with others, and achieve greater happiness and well-being in your personal and professional life.

32: Building Strong Relationships with Extended Family for Optimal Living

Having strong relationships with extended family members can provide a sense of support, belonging, and happiness in our lives. Whether it's through regular family gatherings, holiday celebrations, or simply staying in touch, having strong relationships with extended family can bring a sense of comfort and security to our lives.

In this comprehensive guide to optimal living, we will explore the various aspects of building strong relationships with extended family, and provide tips and strategies to help you deepen your connections with your loved ones and achieve greater happiness in your personal and professional life.

One of the keys to building strong relationships with extended family is understanding and respect for individual differences. Whether it's through different opinions, lifestyles, or beliefs, it's important to recognize and respect the diversity of your extended family members. By embracing these differences, you can create a positive and supportive environment in your relationships and avoid unnecessary conflict and negativity.

Another important aspect of building strong relationships with extended family is effective communication. By being clear, direct, and respectful in your communication, you can foster a sense of understanding and support in your relationships. Additionally, by actively listening to the perspectives and needs of your family members, you can build trust and deepen your connections with others.

It is also essential to make time for your extended family. Whether it's through regular family gatherings, holiday celebrations, or simply staying in touch, making time for your loved ones is essential for maintaining and strengthening your relationships.

In addition to these basic principles, there are many other strategies and techniques that can help you to build strong relationships with extended family. From developing your emotional intelligence and empathy, to practicing forgiveness and resolving conflicts in healthy and effective ways, there are many ways to deepen your connections with your loved ones and achieve greater happiness in your personal and professional life.

So, whether you are looking to build strong relationships with your extended family for the first time, or you are looking to deepen and strengthen your existing relationships, this chapter on building strong relationships with extended family for optimal living is here to help. With its comprehensive guide to family relationships, you will have the tools you need to create meaningful and fulfilling connections with your loved ones, and achieve greater happiness and well-being in your personal and professional life.

33: Building a Strong Community for Optimal Living

Building a strong community is essential for optimal living and can have a profound impact on our happiness, well-being, and sense of belonging. Whether it's through volunteering, participating in community events, or simply connecting with others, having a strong sense of community can help us to feel supported, connected, and fulfilled in our personal and professional lives.

In this comprehensive guide to optimal living, we will explore the various aspects of building a strong community, and provide tips and strategies to help you connect with others and achieve greater happiness in your life.

One of the keys to building a strong community is to be an active and engaged participant. Whether it's through volunteering, participating in community events, or simply connecting with others, it's important to actively seek out opportunities to connect and engage with others. By doing so, you can build relationships, develop a sense of belonging, and gain a deeper understanding of the needs and perspectives of those around you.

Another important aspect of building a strong community is to have a positive and supportive attitude. By being respectful, kind, and empathetic towards others, you can create a positive and supportive environment in your community, and foster greater connections and relationships with others.

It is also essential to participate in community-building activities that are meaningful and relevant to your interests and values. Whether it's through volunteering, participating in community events, or simply connecting with others, it's important to seek out opportunities that align with your personal and professional goals, and that allow you to make a positive impact in your community.

In addition to these basic principles, there are many other strategies and techniques that can help you to build a strong community. From developing your leadership skills and emotional intelligence, to fostering a sense of empathy and compassion for others, there are many ways to deepen your connections with your community and achieve greater happiness and well-being in your life.

So, whether you are looking to build a strong community for

the first time, or you are looking to deepen and strengthen your existing relationships, this chapter on building a strong community for optimal living is here to help. With its comprehensive guide to community building, you will have the tools you need to connect with others, make a positive impact in your community, and achieve greater happiness and well-being in your personal and professional life.

34: Finding Your Purpose in Life for Optimal Living

Finding your purpose in life is an essential aspect of optimal living and can have a profound impact on your happiness, well-being, and sense of fulfillment. Whether it's through work, relationships, community involvement, or personal interests, having a clear sense of purpose can help you to focus your energy, prioritize your goals, and find meaning and satisfaction in your life.

In this comprehensive guide to optimal living, we will explore the various aspects of finding your purpose in life, and provide tips and strategies to help you discover your passions, set meaningful goals, and achieve greater happiness and fulfillment in your personal and professional life.

One of the first steps in finding your purpose in life is to reflect on your values, beliefs, and priorities. Take some time to think about what is truly important to you, and what kind of impact you want to have in the world. This self-reflection will help you to identify your unique talents and strengths, and provide a starting point for discovering your purpose.

Another important aspect of finding your purpose in life is

to explore your passions and interests. Whether it's through taking up a new hobby, volunteering, or pursuing a new career, it's important to actively seek out opportunities to pursue your passions and to develop your skills and abilities. By doing so, you can gain a deeper understanding of your purpose, and begin to see the world in a new and meaningful way.

It is also essential to set meaningful and achievable goals that align with your purpose and priorities. Whether it's through setting career goals, personal goals, or community goals, having a clear sense of direction and purpose can help you to stay motivated, focused, and engaged in your life.

In addition to these basic principles, there are many other strategies and techniques that can help you to find your purpose in life. From developing your emotional intelligence and self-awareness, to pursuing new experiences and learning opportunities, there are many ways to deepen your understanding of your purpose, and to achieve greater happiness and fulfillment in your life.

So, whether you are just starting to explore your purpose in life, or you are looking to deepen and strengthen your existing sense of purpose, this chapter on finding your purpose in life for optimal living is here to help. With its comprehensive guide to purpose-finding, you will have the tools you need to discover your passions, set meaningful goals, and achieve greater happiness and fulfillment in your personal and professional life.

35: Building a Strong Spiritual Foundation for Optimal Living

Building a strong spiritual foundation is an important aspect of optimal living, and can play a significant role in shaping your outlook on life, your values, and your sense of well-being. Whether it's through religious faith, mindfulness practices, or a connection to the natural world, a strong spiritual foundation can provide you with a source of inner strength, comfort, and guidance as you navigate life's challenges and opportunities.

In this comprehensive guide to optimal living, we will explore the various aspects of building a strong spiritual foundation, and provide tips and strategies to help you develop a deeper sense of connection and purpose in your life.

One of the first steps in building a strong spiritual foundation is to reflect on your values and beliefs. Take some time to think about what is truly important to you, and what kind of impact you want to have in the world. This self-reflection will help you to identify your spiritual needs, and provide a starting point for connecting with your inner self and the world around you.

35: BUILDING A STRONG SPIRITUAL FOUNDATION
FOR OPTIMAL LIVING

Another important aspect of building a strong spiritual foundation is to engage in practices that foster spiritual growth and well-being. This may involve regular meditation, prayer, or mindfulness practices, as well as spending time in nature, reading inspiring books, or engaging in acts of kindness and service. By taking steps to nourish your spiritual life, you can develop a deeper sense of connection and purpose, and experience a greater sense of peace and happiness in your life.

It is also essential to seek out supportive communities that can help you to deepen your spiritual practice and provide a source of inspiration and guidance. Whether it's through a religious community, a spiritual group, or simply spending time with like-minded individuals, having a supportive network can help you to stay motivated, focused, and connected to your spiritual path.

In addition to these basic principles, there are many other strategies and techniques that can help you to build a strong spiritual foundation in your life. From exploring different spiritual traditions and practices, to connecting with the natural world and seeking out new learning opportunities, there are many ways to deepen your spiritual life and achieve greater happiness and fulfillment.

So, whether you are just starting to explore spirituality, or you are looking to deepen and strengthen your existing spiritual practice, this chapter on building a strong spiritual foundation for optimal living is here to help. With its comprehensive guide to spiritual growth and well-being, you will have the tools you need to connect with your inner self, build a strong spiritual foundation, and achieve greater happiness and fulfillment in your personal and professional life.

36: Conclusion: Achieving True Happiness Through Optimal Living

In this book, we have explored the many different aspects of optimal living and how they all contribute to achieving true happiness. We have discussed the importance of finding work-life balance, building a strong financial foundation, creating a happy home, building strong parenting skills, building strong relationships with your spouse, friends, extended family, and community, finding your purpose in life, and building a strong spiritual foundation. Each of these aspects is crucial to living a life of happiness and fulfillment.

Achieving true happiness is not a one-time event, but a lifelong journey that requires ongoing effort and attention. It is important to recognize that there will be ups and downs along the way, but the key is to keep moving forward and making progress, no matter how small. The key to success is to take one step at a time and to be patient with yourself.

One of the most important things to remember is that the journey of optimal living is a personal one, and what works for one person may not work for another. The most important thing is to find what works for you and to make it a priority in your life. This may mean making changes to your daily habits, your work situation, your relationships, or any other aspect of your life that is not serving you.

It is also important to remember that happiness is not a destination, but a state of mind. No matter what your circumstances, you have the power to choose happiness and to cultivate it in your life. You can do this by focusing on what is good in your life, and by being grateful for what you have. When you focus on the positive, you will find that your life will become more fulfilling and you will feel happier.

In conclusion, optimal living is a journey of personal growth and self-discovery, and it requires effort, patience, and a willingness to make changes. When you focus on the different aspects of optimal living, you will find that you are able to achieve true happiness, and that your life will be more fulfilling and meaningful. With hard work, determination, and a positive attitude, you can transform your life and achieve true happiness.

So, take the first step today and start your journey towards optimal living. Remember that the journey is worth it, and that you are worth it. You have the power to create a life of happiness and fulfillment, and it all starts with you.

Thank You

As we reach the end of this book, I want to say thanks for reading this book.

I want to get this information out to as many people as possible. If you found this book helpful, I would greatly appreciate you leaving me a review. This helps others find the book as well.

Disclaimer

This document is geared towards providing exact and reliable information in regards to the topic and issue covered. The publication is sold on the idea that the publisher is not required to render an accounting, officially permitted, or otherwise, qualified services. If advice is necessary, legal, financial, medical or professional, a practiced individual in the profession should be ordered.

This information is not presented by a financial or medical practitioner and is for entertainment, educational and informational purposes only. The content is not intended as a substitute for professional medical advice, diagnosis, or treatment. Always seek the advice of your physician or other qualified health care provider with any questions you may have regarding a medical condition. Never disregard professional medical advice or delay in seeking it because of something you have read.

The information provided herein is stated to be truthful and consistent, in that any liability, in terms of inattention or otherwise, by any usage or abuse of any policies, processes, or directions contained within is the solitary and utter responsibility of the recipient reader. Under no circumstances

DISCLAIMER

will any legal responsibility or blame be held against the publisher for any reparation, damages, or monetary loss due to the information herein, either directly or indirectly.